# THE UNTAMED WORLD

# Black Rhinos

E. Melanie Watt

RSVP®

RAINTREE
STECK-VAUGHN
PUBLISHERS

The Steck-Vaughn Company

*Austin, Texas*

Published by Raintree Steck-Vaughn Publishers, an imprint of Steck-Vaughn Company.

**Library of Congress Cataloging-in-Publication Data**
Watt, Melanie.
    Black rhinos / E. Melanie Watt.
       p.    cm. -- (The untamed world)
    Includes bibliographical references (p. 63) and index.
    Summary: Examines the life, environment, habits, and endangered status of the black rhino.
    ISBN 0-8172-4572-3
    1. Black rhinoceros--Juvenile literature.  [1. Black rhinoceros.
2. Rhinoceroses.  3. Endangered species.]  I. Title.  II. Series.
QL737.U63W38      1998
599.66'8--dc21                      97-11464
                                      CIP
                                      AC

Printed and bound in Canada
1234567890  01 00 99 98 97

**Project Editor**
Lauri Seidlitz

**Design and Illustration**
Warren Clark

**Raintree Steck-Vaughn Publishers Editor**
Kathy DeVico

**Copy Editors**
Janice Parker, Leslie Strudwick

**Layout**
Chris Bowerman

**Consultants**
David Cumming is a member of the Zimbabwe Rhino Conservancy Project. The Conservancy is establishing black rhino breeding groups in private conservancies with community outreach programs.

Raoul du Toit is WWF Project Executant for the Zimbabwe Rhino Conservancy Project.

**Acknowledgments**
The publisher wishes to thank Warren Rylands for inspiring this series.

**Photograph Credits**

**Frank S. Balthis**: page 36; **Corel Corporation**: pages cover, 5, 7, 9, 13, 18, 21, 23, 26, 30, 39, 42, 43, 59, 60, 61; **Brian Keating**: page 53; **Tom Stack and Associates**: pages 4 (Roy Toft), 22, 24, 31 (Nancy Adams), 28, 52 (Warren & Genny Garst), 35 (Joe McDonald), 40 (Chip & Jill Isenhart); **Dave Taylor**: pages 12, 15, 20, 33, 34, 41, 46, 54, 56, 57; **U.S. Fish and Wildlife Service**: pages 17 (Maslowski Productions), 29 (John & Karen Hollingsworth); **Visuals Unlimited**: pages 6, 25 (Joe McDonald), 19 (Hal Beral), 27 (David L. Pearson), 32 (A.J. Cunningham), 38 (Ken Lucas).

Every reasonable effort has been made to trace ownership and to obtain permission to reprint copyright material. The publishers would be pleased to have any errors or omissions brought to their attention so that they may be corrected in subsequent printings.

# Contents

# Introduction

**Some people want rhino horns so badly that they risk their lives for them.**

*Opposite: In Africa, the black rhino is the fourth largest land mammal, after elephants, white rhinos, and hippopotamuses.*

Black rhinoceroses, or rhinos, are among the largest land mammals in the world. Although these powerful animals can weigh thousands of pounds (kilograms) and charge at high speeds, they have been hunted to the brink of extinction.

In this book you will discover where black rhinos live, what they eat, and how they raise their young. You will learn about the sounds they make that we cannot hear, and about other ways they may communicate with one another. You will find out why some people risk their lives to get rhino horns. You will also find out why other people risk their lives to save black rhinos from extinction.

This book will help you understand the rhino and its world. You will see what is being done to help save the rhino and what you can do to help.

*Rhinos have poor vision and will sometimes charge things they do not recognize.*

# Features

**Both black and white rhinos are actually gray in color.**

*Opposite: Although some black rhinos have as many as five horns, most have two.*

Many people find it difficult to tell the difference between black and white rhinos. Both rhinos have two horns and are similar in many other ways. The biggest confusion comes from their names. Both black and white rhinos are actually gray in color. Some people think that the white rhino was once called the "wide" rhino, to describe its wide upper lip, but became known as the white rhino. White rhinos are also known as square-lipped rhinos because of the distinct shape of their upper lip. Their lip is designed to help them graze on short grasses. Black rhinos have a pointed upper lip, which allows them to eat parts of trees and shrubs more easily. Black rhinos are also known as hooked-lip rhinos. This lip difference is the easiest way to tell these two species apart. The black rhino also has a shorter head than the white rhino and a swayed back.

*The white rhino's square lip makes it easy to identify. The black rhino has a pointed upper lip.*

# Ancestors

The first rhinos roamed Earth about 50 million years ago. These rhino ancestors did not have horns and looked more like small horses than the rhinos of today. There were many types of rhino ancestors. Some were small, and some were very large. The oldest samples of horned rhinos were found in North America. They lived there 25 to 40 million years ago.

A more recent horned species of rhino lived in Europe and Asia. These rhinos had many different sizes and shapes of horns. Some rhinos had only one horn, but others had several horns. Some of these early rhinos even had two horns beside each other. The rhino species that are alive today have been on Earth for about 3 million years.

*Scientists think that the largest land mammal that ever lived was part of the rhino family. This animal was known as the* Indricotherium *and was about 28 feet (8.5 m) long.*

# Classification

Today there are five species of rhinos in the world. There are differences between these species, but there are also many similarities. They all have large heads; huge bodies; short necks; short, thick legs; and either one or two horns. Rhinos also have small eyes; thick, wrinkled skin; and three toes on each foot. All rhinos have poor vision, but they can smell and hear very well. If threatened, they may charge at whatever is disturbing them, but since they have such poor eyesight, they may not always hit their target.

In rhino species that have only one horn, the horn sits over the nose area. In the species with two horns, the second horn sits above the eyes. The Greater Indian rhino and the Javan rhino have only one horn. The Sumatran rhino has two horns, but its front horn is so small that it is often hard to see. The white rhino and the black rhino both have two horns.

*The Greater Indian rhino has only one horn. Although it is highly endangered, it is the most commonly seen of the Asian rhino species.*

# Rhinos of the World

Unless you are an expert, you may not know how to tell one species of rhino from another. Look at the clues on this page to see if you can spot the differences.

## African Rhinos

**Black Rhino**
- Two horns
- Usually weighs less than 2,860 pounds (1,300 kg)
- **Browser**

**White Rhino**
- Two horns
- Usually weighs less than 7,700 pounds (3,500 kg)
- **Grazer**

# Asian Rhinos

### Sumatran Rhino
- Two horns (front one is very small)
- Usually weighs less than 1,870 pounds (850 kg)
- Has hair on its body
- Browser

### Greater Indian Rhino
- One horn
- Usually weighs less than 4,620 pounds (2,100 kg)
- Bumpy skin looks like armor
- Browser

### Javan Rhino
- One horn
- Usually weighs less than 4,180 pounds (1,900 kg)
- Scaly-looking skin looks like armor
- Browser

# Subspecies

Every known species and subspecies of animal has been given a Latin name. This means that biologists from all over the world who speak different languages and have different common names for animals will understand exactly which animal is being discussed. There is only one species of black rhino in the world, so the Latin name used for all black rhinos is the same: *Diceros bicornis*. Each word following *Diceros bicornis* describes the subspecies of black rhino to which the animal belongs. Biologists have a more difficult time deciding how subspecies should be divided than they do deciding on species. Some scientists have suggested there may be as few as two black rhino subspecies, and some have suggested there are as many as 16. Recently many

scientists agreed that all black rhinos fit into one of four subspecies. These subspecies are found in different parts of the rhino's range. The table below gives the Latin name of each subspecies followed by the number of individuals that are thought to be alive in the wild.

*The black rhino is found in southwestern, south central, and eastern Africa. A few live in the rain forests of Cameroon.*

| BLACK RHINO SUBSPECIES | |
| --- | --- |
| **Latin Name** | **Population** |
| *Diceros bicornis bicornis* | 611 |
| *Diceros bicornis longipes* | 27 |
| *Diceros bicornis michaeli* | 492 |
| *Diceros bicornis minor* | 1,420 |

# A Rhino Quiz

Try this quiz to see how much you know about rhinos.
Are the following statements true or false?
The answers are at the bottom of this page.

**1.** The best way to tell a black rhino from a white rhino is by its color.

**2.** Black rhinos are bigger than white rhinos.

**3.** There are five species of rhinos alive today.

**4.** There are less than 3,000 black rhinos alive in the wild.

**5.** All rhinos have two horns.

**6.** Scent is an important part of communication among black rhinos.

**Answers:**

1) **False.** They are both a similar gray color.

2) **False.** White rhinos are the bigger rhinos.

3) **True.** White, black, Indian, Javan, and Sumatran rhinos.

4) **True.** Only about 2,550 black rhinos are left in the world today.

5) **False.** The white, black, and Sumatran rhinos have two horns, while the Indian and Javan rhinos have only one.

6) **True.** Black rhinos rarely make direct contact with one another. Instead they communicate through scent markings.

# Size

All rhino species are known for their size and powerful build, as well as for their horns. White rhinos are large even by rhino standards, with adult males weighing 5,000 to 7,700 pounds (2,268 to 3,493 kg). The weight of a black rhino depends partly on its subspecies. A black rhino usually weighs between 1,750 and 4,400 pounds (800 and 2,000 kg). Males and females weigh about the same. The black rhino stands about 60 inches (150 cm) tall at the shoulders. Its head and body length is usually about 120 inches (300 cm) long. Its tail is about 20 inches (50 cm) long, with bristles on the end.

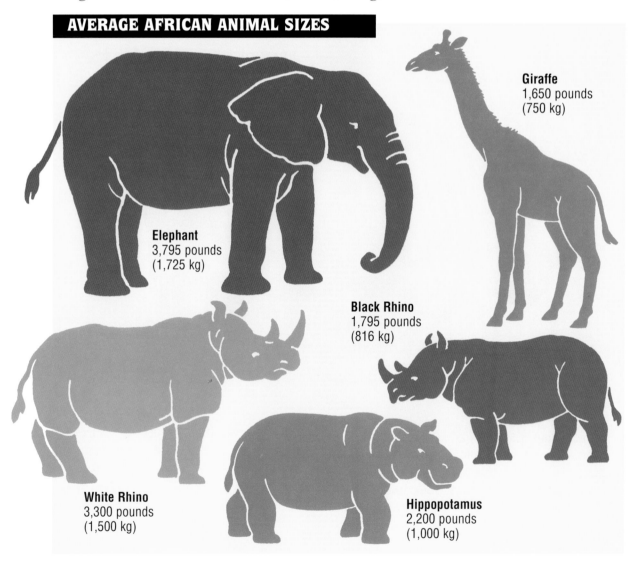

**AVERAGE AFRICAN ANIMAL SIZES**

**Giraffe**
1,650 pounds
(750 kg)

**Elephant**
3,795 pounds
(1,725 kg)

**Black Rhino**
1,795 pounds
(816 kg)

**White Rhino**
3,300 pounds
(1,500 kg)

**Hippopotamus**
2,200 pounds
(1,000 kg)

# Skin

A rhino's skin has often been described as its armor. On its hindquarters, where the skin is thickest, a black rhino's skin is about 0.5 inches (1.3 cm) thick. Its skin is harder on the soles of its feet than anywhere else on its body. An adult black rhino's skin is almost hairless. Black rhinos have many **parasites** that feed on their skin. One type of parasite causes sores around the shoulder area, where it is most difficult for rhinos to get at when rolling. Almost every wild rhino has this kind of parasite. Rhinos may help get rid of their skin parasites by wallowing in the mud. The mud on their skin helps prevent flies from biting. In addition, when the mud dries and falls off, it takes many parasites with it.

*Black rhinos are usually a gray color, but they often take on the color of the earth when they take mud or dust baths.*

## LIFE SPAN

In captivity black rhinos may live to be more than 30 years old. One rhino was still alive after 45 years in captivity. Without protection from humans, it is unlikely that many reach this age in the wild. It is not known how old rhinos can get in the wild. It is possible that wild rhinos that are undisturbed by humans may live longer than zoo animals.

# Special Adaptations

Rhinos have many special features that help them survive the challenges of their environment. However, some of their senses are not well developed compared to other animals. These senses are not as important to the rhino's survival.

## Hearing

Rhinos have very good hearing. They can turn their large, cup-shaped ears to hear sounds coming from different directions.

## Smell

The rhino's sense of smell is excellent. The size of its nasal passages is even bigger than the size of its brain. Rhinos use their sense of smell to help them avoid predators. Wind direction plays an important role in their success. If the wind is blowing from the predator's direction toward the rhino, it can smell the predator a long way away. However, if the wind is blowing the opposite way, the predator may not be noticed. The rhino's sense of smell is also extremely important in communicating with other rhinos.

## Sight

Compared to their other senses, rhino eyesight is poor. They are nearsighted and may be able to see well only for about 100 feet (30 m). They do not seem to see much beyond this distance unless an object is moving.

## Lip

The black rhino's upper lip is **prehensile**, which means it is specially designed to grip objects such as branches and leaves. It is pointed and very flexible, a bit like a short elephant trunk.

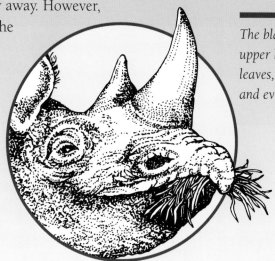

*The black rhino's prehensile upper lip helps it browse for leaves, branches, long grasses, and even fruit.*

# Horns

Rhino horns are made of hollow fibers of **keratin**, which look like hair. Unlike other animal horns, they do not have a bony center core, so they tend to fray and wear down. Rhinos keep their horns sharp by rubbing them on trees or rocks. Rubbing on rocks wears their horns down more than rubbing on wood. Too much rock rubbing can wear a rhino's horn down too much. If a rhino's horn gets knocked off, it will regrow about 2 inches (5 cm) per year.

Females often have longer horns than males. The black rhino's front horn, over its nose area, is usually bigger than the horn farther back on its face. The front horn is usually about 20 inches (51 cm) long in adults. The record for the longest horn is 53.5 inches (136 cm). Almost all black rhinos have only two horns, but some have the beginnings of a third horn a bit farther back. There have even been reports of black rhinos with five horns.

# Legs and Feet

A rhino has very strong, thick legs with three toes on each foot. The toes are cushioned by a soft pad on the bottom of the foot. The middle toe of each foot carries most of the rhino's weight. Its front legs carry more weight than its back legs. The back feet are used to push the rhino forward. Although a black rhino may look slow and clumsy, it can be very fast and agile. When a black rhino charges at something, it can reach speeds of 31 miles per hour (50 kph). It can keep up a fast run for a long distance without stopping.

*Rhino horns can be quite heavy. On average each black rhino carries about 8 pounds (3.6 kg) of horn on its face.*

# The Crash

**A group of rhinos is called a crash.**

*Opposite: Adult rhinos come together briefly for mating, but generally they live alone.*

Black rhinos spend their time alone, with a few exceptions. Several rhinos will share a water hole and may wallow in the mud at the same time. Mothers and young stay together for several years and may be temporarily joined by a male during the mating period. Until they are adults, young that have left their mothers will often group together, or they may occasionally rejoin their mother. Sometimes even adult males will form a temporary group. The largest group of black rhinos reported was made up of 13 individuals. A group of rhinos is called a **crash**.

*Mothers and calves stay together for several years.*

# Communication

When they meet, white rhino males tend to size each other up and then part company. The males will often stand with their noses together and then back off and wipe their horns on the ground. This ritual may help them decide which one is bigger and stronger.

Unlike white rhinos, black rhinos rarely have these confrontations. Black rhinos have larger **home ranges** than white rhinos, so they do not usually meet up with other rhinos. Black rhino males try to avoid one another. They may do this by communicating with scent marks in areas where their home ranges overlap.

Both black and white rhino males will occasionally have serious fights. They will use their horns to jab upward and stab their opponents. Both animals can be injured severely in these contests.

*When a rhino is afraid, it will often lift and curl its tail. It will then usually run away.*

## Sounds

Calves and mothers call to each other with high-pitched mewing sounds. Calves may also make a soft bleating noise when they are separated from their mother. If a calf is suddenly frightened, it may also make a loud squealing sound. Adult black rhinos often snort at each other during confrontations. When they are fighting, they scream, roar, and grunt. Adult rhinos also make a puffing noise when they approach others.

Scientists have found that rhinos also make noises that are too low for humans to hear. These very low sounds can travel over long distances. More research is needed before scientists will know if these sounds are used by rhinos to communicate with one another.

## Markings

Scent is very important in black rhino communication. Rhinos scent mark their own home ranges in several ways. Adult males tend to scrape their back feet in their **dung** so that they leave a stronger scent trail when they walk. They often return to specific areas beside their trails to leave their dung. Fresh dung on the pile helps communicate their presence in the area.

Adult males also walk around the edges of their home range daily, spraying urine on rocks, bushes, and other vegetation. They spray their urine along the trails they use to get to and from their water holes. They most often spray at areas where several rhinos' home ranges overlap. The rhinos can tell individuals apart from their scent. They will react less aggressively to the scent markings made by their neighbors than they will to the scents of unknown rhinos.

Females also spray their urine when they are ready to breed, but the spray is not directed at anything. The scent of a female's urine tells males in the area that she is ready to mate.

## Body Language

When black rhinos approach each other aggressively, they usually walk in a stiff-legged manner, taking short steps. They will often stick their tails up in the air as they move. They may also swing their heads, stab the air with their horns, and paw the ground. When a rhino is about to attack, it lowers its head and flattens its ears. It may make short, incomplete charges, or it may use its horns to try to make contact and hurt the other rhino.

*Before rhinos charge, they often paw the ground.*

# Rhino Calves

**A female black rhino gives birth to and raises one calf at a time.**

*Opposite: A rhino calf has a patch of thick skin on its nose where its horn will grow.*

A young rhino is called a calf. A female black rhino gives birth to and raises one calf at a time. There seems to be an equal chance of the calf being a male or a female. The **gestation period** for rhinos is about 465 days. When females are pregnant, they may either get very aggressive toward males or just avoid them. When a male first approaches a female rhino to breed, she will often be hostile, even to the point of attacking him. She may chase him off with short charges until she is ready to mate. During the mating period, an adult male and female form a temporary group. If the female still has a calf, the three of them can sometimes be found in a group around this time, or the male may chase the young rhino away from its mother.

*A female will often chase off a male when he first approaches her to mate. However, when she is ready, the rhinos form a temporary group for the mating period.*

# Development

## 1 Month – 4 Months

Rhinos will go into hiding when they are about to give birth. After a black rhino calf is born, the mother often licks it. It can stand up when it is about an hour old, and it can walk within 2 hours. A black rhino calf usually follows its mother wherever she goes. This is different from a white rhino calf, which walks a few steps ahead of its mother. This difference may be due to their habitat. Black rhino mothers clear a path through the bushes as they walk, making it easier for their young to follow them. White rhinos usually walk through grass, so this path clearing is not important. Sometimes a black rhino mother will leave her calf in bushes or another hiding place while she goes to drink or browse.

Black rhino calves weigh between 60 and 100 pounds (27 and 45 kg) at birth. During the first 4 months, a calf gains about 2.8 pounds (1.3 kg) per day. It is born with thick skin on the end of its nose, where the nose horn will eventually grow, and a white patch where the other horn will grow. It usually suckles milk from its mother within a few hours of birth. Rhino calves will suckle while their mother is standing up or lying down. When they are about a week and a half old, calves may also start nibbling at plants. By the time calves are about three weeks old, they have already learned to wallow in the mud.

*A calf can walk within 2 hours of being born.*

## 4 Months – 2 Years

Although it begins to eat more and more plants, the rhino calf may continue to suckle milk from its mother for 1 to 2 years. A young rhino will stay with its mother even after it is **weaned**.

When a calf is four months old, its nose horn is about 1.6 inches (4 cm) long. After five months the second horn begins to show. When it is six months old the second horn is about 0.4 inches (1 cm) long, and by eight months it is about 1 inch (3 cm) long. After eight months the first horn is about 3 inches (7.5 cm) long.

## 2 Years – 7 Years

When a calf is two to five years old, it is often forced to leave its mother either when the mother mates, or when a new calf is born. The calf may then join other calves or a single female until it is full grown and lives on its own. Even after the birth of the next calf, a young rhino may still occasionally return to join its mother, especially if the youngster is female. By three years of age, a calf is almost as big as its mother but will not be full grown until it is about seven years old. Female black rhinos do not usually have calves until they are more than four-and-a-half years old.

*A black rhino calf usually follows its mother. Her large bulk clears a path through the trees and bushes of their environment, making it easier for the calf to walk.*

# Habitat

**Black rhinos are sometimes found on the slopes of mountains, as high up as 9,000 feet (2,743 m).**

_Opposite: Most black rhinos prefer to live on the edges of wooded areas, where cover is available._

_Rhinos like habitats where they can take mud and dust baths to help them control parasites that live on their skin._

Black rhinos can be found in many different types of African habitats, from forests to deserts. Unlike white rhinos, which prefer open grasslands, black rhinos are most commonly found on the edges of wooded areas or in other areas where there is some cover. Black rhinos prefer regions that are not too dry and not too hot and humid. This may be because these areas have more of the food they like to eat.

Black rhinos are sometimes found on the slopes of mountains, as high up as 9,000 feet (2,743 m). During the heat of the day, black rhinos like shaded areas. At night they may use more open areas. In habitats with water and more bush and tree cover, black rhinos live closer together.

# Home Ranges

Black rhinos usually stay within their own home range. Except for dominant males, their range can overlap with those of other rhinos. Rhinos must live near water, and because water can be scarce in their habitat, several rhinos will often use the same water hole. Rhinos know which other rhinos are their neighbors. This helps them to avoid fighting. Male rhinos tend to fight only with new males coming into their area. The size of a home range depends upon the characteristics of the habitat. In areas where there is more to eat and plenty of water, a home range may only be 1 square mile (2.6 sq km), but when there is less to eat it may be as big as 51 square miles (133 sq km). Within its home range, a black rhino has favorite spots that it uses more often than others. During the day a rhino tends to be less active and use only a small area within its home range. At night it is usually more active, using more of its home range.

*Rhinos are tolerant of one another at shared water holes.*

*Rhinos do not have to travel as far to find food or water during the rainy season.*

# Seasonal Activities

Rhinos may use different parts of their home range during different seasons. During the dry season, rhinos must stay close to a water hole, usually within 3 miles (5 km). They also tend to eat more plants that store water in their roots and stems. A rhino will sometimes walk miles (kilometers) to find a new water source in times of drought. However, a rhino will not migrate permanently out of its home range, even if its water disappears. In the rainy season, black rhinos can travel farther away from a reliable source of water.

Rhinos can breed and give birth at any time of year. However, in some areas breeding is more common at certain times. In Kenya, for example, black rhino breeding is most common from September to November. In South Africa it is more common from April to July.

29

# Daily Routine

Rhinos are creatures of habit. They like to use the same trails through the bush or savanna until their routes are well worn. Most rhinos eat early in the morning. Then they rest throughout the hottest part of the day. Rhinos often rest in the shade, but some have been seen dozing in the hot sun. In the late afternoon a rhino will cool off in a mud wallow and start to eat again.

Rhinos usually nap standing up but will lie on their stomachs for longer rests. If they lie down to sleep, they stand up frequently. They move around, as if they need to stretch their legs and muscles. Rhinos are more vulnerable to predators when they are lying down, so their mid-nap stretches likely help keep them prepared in case of danger. Black rhinos usually sleep alone, except for mothers and calves.

*Rhinos, like many animals, rest during the hottest part of the day.*

*A rhino needs mud or water to keep cool and help it get rid of parasites.*

# On the Track of a Rhino

Black rhinos are so rare that you would be lucky to see one in the wild. In some protected areas you may see some of these signs that rhinos are in the region:

1. **Tracks:** Look for large, three-toed tracks that are shaped something like the clubs in a deck of cards.

2. **Evidence of feeding:** Watch for broken branches, seedlings pulled up by their roots, or the leaves and branches less than 1.2 inches (3 cm) in diameter nipped off.

3. **Mud wallows:** Signs of rhinos can often be found around patches of wet mud along game trails in rhino territories. These muddy areas often have troughs left by rolling rhinos. The distinct rhino footprints can be found at the soft edges of these wallows.

4. **Fresh dung on a dung pile:** Much of the pile may have been spread when the rhino scraped its back feet through the dung.

# Food

**Black rhinos tend to eat alone.**

*Opposite: Rhinos use their upper lip like an elephant's trunk to grab their food.*

All rhinos are **herbivores**, which means they eat plants. Like many herbivores, rhinos digest their food slowly. Black rhinos are big animals that need to eat a lot of food each day, so they tend to eat alone. This way they are not competing with other rhinos for food. Black rhinos and white rhinos eat different types of plants. White rhinos are grazers, which means they eat mostly short grasses. Black rhinos are browsers, which means they eat parts of trees and shrubs instead of short grass. Black rhinos do not just eat one type of plant. What they eat changes depending on the season and on what is available in an individual rhino's area.

*Black rhinos will eat long grass, but they prefer trees, leaves, and shrubs.*

# What They Eat

Black rhinos browse on woody shrubs, small trees, and plants with broad leaves. They will also eat fruit. They sometimes take in grass when they are eating other plants, but grass is not an important part of their diet. If they are in open grasslands, they will occasionally feed on clumps of long grass. After a fire has been through an area, rhinos have even been seen picking out charred twigs to eat. They need to eat a lot of food. Black rhinos usually eat more than 51 pounds (23 kg) of vegetation each day. To get all this food, they eat many different species of plants. In some regions, black rhinos are known to eat up to 191 different species of plants. Rhinos can even eat plants that have special bad-tasting chemicals in them that protect them from being eaten by other animals.

*Black rhinos usually eat more than 51 pounds (23 kg) of vegetation each day.*

# How and When They Eat

A black rhino uses its upper lip to pull off bits of trees and other plants. It even uses its lip to pull fruit out of trees. By stepping on small trees, it brings the higher branches into reach. It also uses its horn to pull branches down. In more open areas, a black rhino may eat small, newly growing trees. It pulls these saplings right out of the ground with its mouth.

Black rhinos eat mainly in the morning and evening. During the hottest part of the day, they are fairly inactive as they try to keep cool.

*A black rhino's prehensile upper lip is an important adaptation to help it grasp and eat food.*

*In the rainy season, rhinos can go without drinking water for several days.*

# Water

Rhinos must stay near water, especially during hot weather. When it is hot and dry, they must find water to drink at least once a day, so they usually stay within 3 miles (5 km) of a water hole or other source of water. In some desert areas rhinos may have to travel up to 9 miles (15 km) away from water to their feeding grounds. They travel most of these long distances at night. They find water by using their front feet to dig holes up to 20 inches (50 cm) deep. When it is not the hot season, rhinos may go without drinking water for up to 5 days.

Black rhinos also wallow in mud and water. This helps get rid of parasites and cools them down. After they get out of muddy water, rhinos stay cool for more than an hour as the mud dries.

# Wildlife Biologists Talk About Black Rhinos

## Dr. Esmond Bradley Martin

*"Because of the present demand for rhino horn and hide—and the high prices being paid for them—I fear that present conservation methods are not adequate to ensure a future for rhinos outside zoos or a few isolated reserves."*

Dr. Martin was vice-chairman of the African Elephant and Rhino Specialist Group of the International Union for Conservation of Nature (IUCN). He has investigated the trade in rhino parts throughout Asia and Africa.

## Dr. Mark Atkinson

*"The rhinoceros, throughout its historical range, has been hunted for its horn and is now on the brink of extinction as a result."*

Dr. Atkinson is a wildlife veterinarian from Zimbabwe, where he worked for the Department of National Parks and Wildlife Management on rhino conservation projects.

## Malcolm Penny

*"Four out of the five species of rhinoceroses in the world are in real danger of becoming extinct before the end of this century. The single exception is the white rhinoceros in South Africa."*

Malcolm Penny is a zoologist and a producer of nature films. He has traveled throughout Africa and India.

# Competition

**The rhino's most dangerous competitors are people.**

Adult rhinos have few enemies. Although they are very powerful and equipped with dangerous horns, male black rhinos rarely fight with other males. The rhino's most dangerous competitors are people. They destroy habitat and have hunted rhinos to the edge of extinction. Poachers make so much money from selling rhino horns for medicine and knife handles that they will risk their lives to kill rhinos.

*Opposite: Very few animals are a threat to the powerful rhino.*

*Rhinos may greet each other by bumping heads.*

# Competing with Other Black Rhinos

Female black rhinos are not usually aggressive toward each other. When they meet they may bump each other with their heads or with the sides of their horns, but then they usually walk away. When male rhinos meet other rhinos, they are not usually as calm. When two males meet, they may snort, paw the ground, sweep their heads back and forth, and push their horns in the air. Then they might make short charges that stop before they reach each other. After a tense standoff, one of them usually walks away.

Usually male rhinos will not attack one another, since the newest animal to the area or the animal that is not as strong will back away. When male rhinos do fight, it is usually the male that lives in the area that attacks the new rhino. He lowers his head, flattens his ears, and makes a screaming groan sound. He might try to club or stab the other rhino with his horn. Adult males have been known to attack young calves, especially during mating periods.

*Serious competition between rhinos is rare. Black rhinos will walk away from confrontations.*

# Relationships with Other Animals

White rhinos and black rhinos are sometimes found in the same areas. When this happens there is little competition between the two species. The two species may even use the same communal dung heap. Black rhinos are browsers, so they do not need to compete for food with the grazing white rhinos.

Adult rhinos are rarely attacked by other animals. Young black rhinos are sometimes killed by hyenas and lions. The mother rhinos protect their young and will even threaten or charge a lion. One researcher reported that a mother rhino had killed a lion to defend her calf. Lions will attack adult rhinos, but this is not very common. There have also been reports of adult rhinos being killed by elephants and crocodiles, but this is also rare. In general, people are the only real enemies of wild rhinos.

*Mother rhinos will threaten and charge any danger to protect their calves.*

*Birds called oxpeckers help rhinos by eating the parasites on their skin.*

# Teamwork

Black rhinos are often seen with small birds sitting on their backs. These birds, called oxpeckers, help the rhinos by eating the parasites on their skin. The rhinos have so many parasites that they provide a continuous source of food for the birds. Oxpeckers also warn the rhinos of approaching danger. The birds can see much better and farther than the rhinos, and they make loud calls when they are alarmed.

Sometimes black rhinos feed near buffalo. This feeding habit also may help protect them against unseen dangers. The buffalo has much better vision than the rhino and will see a predator long before the rhino does.

# Competing with Humans

Humans are the black rhino's most dangerous enemy. Rhinos can also be a threat to people. Usually black rhinos will run away from danger, but sometimes they will approach slowly or charge toward it. Although many rhino charges never result in contact, those that do can kill or seriously hurt people. Black rhinos tend to be more dangerous than white rhinos, mainly because of the areas in which they prefer to live. Humans are less likely to have a surprise encounter with a white rhino living on the open grasslands than a black rhino living in a partially wooded area, where it is more difficult to see. A surprised rhino may charge humans directly and will even charge and badly damage vehicles. There have also been reports of black rhinos charging campfires.

*It is a myth that people can avoid a rhino's charge by stepping aside like a matador. Despite their poor eyesight and large size, rhinos are fast and agile. If they really want to hit their target, they can.*

Although the German engraver Albrecht Dürer had never seen a rhinoceros, his famous woodcut engraving was surprisingly accurate. He based his work on descriptions from explorers. The only big difference was the small horn on the rhino's back.

# *Folklore*

Wildlife plays an important role in African folklore. For centuries black and white rhinos have been part of the folklore of many different African cultures. Stories often focus on the rhino's large size. Some stories do not show the rhino in a positive way. These stories sometimes focus on the rhino's reputed bad temper and laziness. The tales often use rhinos as an example of what happens if people have these qualities. In folktales, the rhino often loses out to the bigger elephant or to other animals that are considered to be smarter than the rhino. Rhinos are often shown as being stupid or easily fooled.

*Many people believe that tales of the unicorn actually describe the rhino. Like the rhino, the unicorn's horn was said to have magical powers.*

# Folklore History

In spite of its poor reputation in many folktales, rhinos are also thought to have healing properties. Unfortunately for the rhinos, it is their body parts that are thought to be powerful medicines. Their horns, hide, and other body parts have been used for centuries in parts of Africa and Asia.

In Africa, rhino horn has not commonly been used for medicines except by the Zulus in South Africa. They use both the horn and the hide to treat illnesses. African use of rhino horn is only a small part of its worldwide use.

Rhino horn has long played a very important role in traditional Asian medicines. These medicines were once made from the horns only of the Javan, Sumatran, and Indian rhinos. When these species became less common, African rhino horn was used instead. Asians still prefer to use horns from local rhinos when possible. The increase in the use of black and white rhino horn increased rhino poaching throughout Africa.

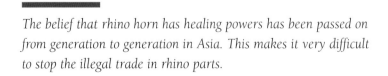

*The belief that rhino horn has healing powers has been passed on from generation to generation in Asia. This makes it very difficult to stop the illegal trade in rhino parts.*

# Myths vs. Facts

**A rhino's skin is so thick that it is bulletproof.**

Although rhino skin is thick, it is not bulletproof. This myth originated because of an early engraving of an Indian rhino by a German artist. The engraving made the rhino look like its skin was made of metal. The artist thought that the rhino's skin was made like a coat of armor, with rivets to hold it in place.

**Rhino horn is a powerful medicine.**

Rhino horn is used as a traditional medicine in parts of Asia and Africa. It is often ground into a powder and mixed with other ingredients to cure a variety of ailments. Scientists in Switzerland have reported that rhino horn has no real healing qualities, but Chinese scientists have reported that it helps cool fever if huge amounts are used.

**Rhinos are lazy and slow.**

Rhinos spend much of their time eating, and when undisturbed they usually move slowly throughout their feeding areas. In the hot midday sun they may rest. Their slow movements might make them appear lazy, but when they are nervous or angry, they can run at speeds up to 31 miles per hour (50 kph).

# Folktales

In folktales from different cultures throughout Africa, rhinos are often portrayed as being nearsighted, slow animals with bad tempers. The rhino is usually shown as the loser in competitions with other species, especially elephants. Many folktales try to explain characteristics of the rhino that are different from other animals, such as its wrinkled skin. Here are a few tales that you might enjoy:

## Foolish Rhinos

"**The Tug-of-War**" is a Ndebele story about a hare that tricks a hippopotamus and a rhinoceros into having a tug-of-war with each other without the two bigger animals knowing what is happening.

Greaves, Nick. *When Hippo Was Hairy and Other Tales from Africa*. Hauppauge, New York: Barron's Educational Series, 1988.

*Rhinos for Lunch and Elephants for Supper!* is based on a Maasai tale about a voice from a cave that shouts, "I eat rhinos for lunch and elephants for supper! Come in if you dare!" All the animals, including the rhino, are afraid of meeting an animal big enough to eat these two huge animals. Most of the animals run away in fear without investigating the source of the voice.

Mollel, Tololwa. *Rhinos for Lunch and Elephants for Supper!* Toronto: Oxford University Press, 1991.

## Bad-Mannered Rhinos

*How the Rhinoceros Got His Skin*, first published in 1902, explains how rhinos got their wrinkled skin. In this story a rhino's bad manners result in it being tricked into wearing an itchy coat that it cannot take off.

Kipling, Rudyard. *How the Rhinoceros Got His Skin (Just So Stories)*. London: Macmillan Children's Books, 1985.

# Why Stories

**"Why Rhino Scatters His Dung"** is a Batonka fable describing a dung-piling contest between an elephant and a rhino. The angry elephant beats up the rhino for winning, and the rhino learns to kick down his dung heap to make it look smaller.

Greaves, Nick. *When Hippo Was Hairy and Other Tales from Africa.* Hauppauge, New York: Barron's Educational Series, 1988.

**"The Lost Quill"** is another fable that describes why rhinos scatter their dung. In this Ndebele story, the rhino thinks he has eaten a borrowed porcupine quill and kicks his dung around to find it.

Greaves, Nick. *When Hippo Was Hairy and Other Tales from Africa.* Hauppauge, New York: Barron's Educational Series, 1988.

**"Why the Giraffe Has a Long Neck"** is an East African fable that explains why the rhino has such a bad temper. A rhino and a giraffe decide they both want long necks to reach up to the treetops. Rhino is late for the meeting with the witch doctor, so he misses out on the special neck-growing potion.

Greaves, Nick. *When Hippo Was Hairy and Other Tales from Africa.* Hauppauge, New York: Barron's Educational Series, 1988.

# Black Rhino Distribution

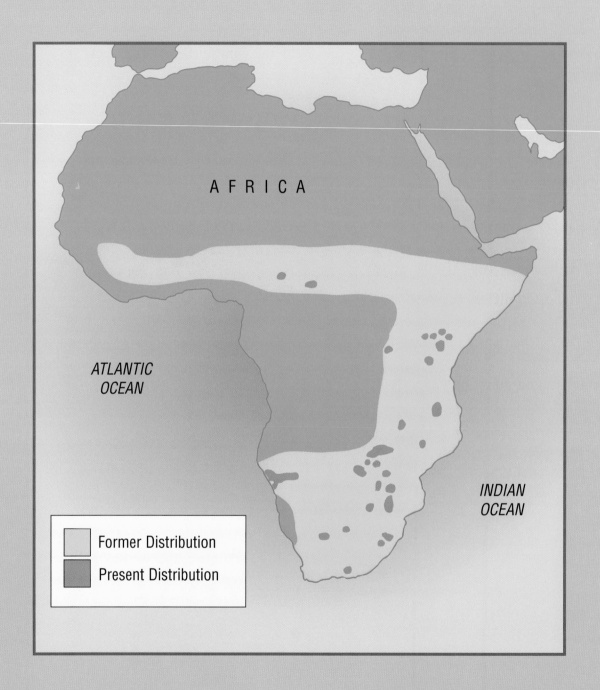

AFRICA

ATLANTIC
OCEAN

INDIAN
OCEAN

Former Distribution

Present Distribution

# Status

**Ninety-five percent of Africa's black rhinos were killed between 1970 and 1994.**

Until recently black rhinos were relatively common in Africa. Ninety-five percent of Africa's black rhinos were killed between 1970 and 1994. Most were killed for their horns, which are used to make traditional medicines and knife handles. Black rhinos are not the only rhino species facing extinction. Including all five species of rhinos, there are only about 12,000 left in the wild.

**Poaching** is the cause of the rhino decline. Researchers believe that 90 percent of all adult rhino deaths are caused by poachers killing them for their horns. After the poachers have cut off the horn, the rest of the rhino is not usually used and is left to rot in the sun.

## RHINO POPULATIONS

| Species | Latin Name | Population |
| --- | --- | --- |
| Sumatran or hairy rhino | *Dicerorhinus sumatrensis* | 450–800 |
| Greater Indian rhino | *Rhinoceros unicornis* | 2,000 |
| Javan rhino | *Rhinoceros sondaicus* | less than 75 |
| Black rhino | *Diceros bicornis* | 2,550 |
| White rhino | *Ceratotherium simum* | 6,780 |

# Decline in Population

In 1970 there were thought to be about 65,000 black rhinos living in the wild. At that time it was the most common species of rhino. By 1993 there were only about 2,550 black rhinos left. The countries with the largest populations of black rhinos are South Africa, with approximately 900, and Namibia, with less than 600.

Other rhino species are in the same situation. The World Conservation Union (IUCN) classifies the southern subspecies of the white rhino as **vulnerable**, and the northern subspecies, which is in even more danger of extinction, as **endangered**. It lists the other four species of rhinos, including the black rhino, as endangered. The Javan rhino is considered to be the rarest large mammal in the world. Conservation groups are working hard to protect the remaining rhinos of all species. Rhinos are now thought to be **extirpated** in Central African Republic, Chad, Ethiopia, Rwanda, Sudan, and Uganda. In Angola, Cameroon, Mozambique, Tanzania, and Zambia there are very few, if any, rhinos left.

*Poachers often chop off rhino horns and leave the rest of the animal to rot. Sometimes their feet are also chopped off to make souvenirs for tourists.*

# The Trade in Rhino Horn

Rhino horn is often used as an ingredient in many traditional Chinese medicines. For thousands of years, rhino horn has been used in medicines to treat problems that include fever, convulsions, strokes, and even nosebleeds. The horn is ground up, made into pills or other medications, and sold to Asian communities around the world. This is a huge business. Between 1990 and 1992, more than 100,000 items made from rhino products were exported from China to about 30 different countries. The price of rhino horn varies depending on the country and the year. In the mid-1980s, powder or scrapings from black rhino horn were selling for about U.S. $4,990 per pound ($11,000 per kg) in Singapore.

Rhino horn is not only used to make medicine, but also to make dagger handles in Yemen. In the 1970s many people in Yemen became wealthy because of the oil business. During the 1970s they bought so many daggers with rhino horn handles that thousands of rhinos were killed. The cost of rhino horn increased dramatically. By 1979 it cost 21 times as much to buy rhino horn as it did in 1971. In the 1980s about 4,400 pounds (2,000 kg) of rhino horn were being shipped to Yemen every year. Pressure from conservation groups helped slow the killing for dagger handles. By 1993 less than 220 pounds (100 kg) of rhino horn were brought into Yemen. Rhinos are still being poached for their horns, even though there are very few rhinos left.

*During the height of the rhino trade, tourists could purchase rhino skulls when visiting Africa.*

# Protecting Rhinos

Conservation groups from all over the world are trying to protect the last remaining rhinos. Some **dehorning** programs have been successful in reducing poaching, but they alone will not solve the problem. Other conservation projects involve moving rhinos to well-protected preserve areas that can be better patrolled by armed guards and antipoaching teams. These teams are well armed, and rhino poachers risk death to make their profits. Conservation projects also involve protecting the rhino's natural habitat.

Another important goal of conservation efforts has been to decrease the trade of rhino products. This includes undercover investigations to catch the people who continue to buy rhino products from poachers. One of the most effective ways to protect rhinos is through education. Conservation education tries to convince people not to buy medicines, daggers, and other products that are made from rhino horn. Poachers and others who share the rhino's environment can learn that rhinos are worth more alive than dead, if they are allowed to share the benefits. These benefits include jobs and profits through nature tourism, parks, and wildlife management.

*In the eyes of a poacher, the rhino's horn is its most important feature. Dehorning programs discourage poachers because they remove the poachers' main reason for hunting rhinos.*

# *Viewpoints*

## Should rhinos be dehorned to try to keep them safe from poachers?

Dehorning projects are sometimes carried out as part of larger conservation efforts to save the black rhino. These projects cause much debate. Individual rhinos are drugged, and 70 to 80 percent of their horn is sawed off. Removing a rhino's horn makes it much less valuable to poachers and thereby helps protect the rhino from being killed. The dehorned area is smoothed down before the animal awakens and is released. Many people think that this procedure interferes with the rhinos too much, while others think that it is worth it to discourage poachers.

**PRO**

**1** Rhinos with horns are poached even in areas with good law enforcement. Removing horns is the best way to protect rhinos.

**2** Rhinos sometimes lose their horns in the wild and regrow them over several years. Studies have shown that rhinos can still successfully breed, raise young, and hold territories after they have lost their horns.

**3** Many rhinos have been dehorned and drugged several times over several years and seem to have no side effects. During Zimbabwe's black rhino project, poaching decreased and the black rhino population increased.

**CON**

**1** By improving law enforcement in poaching areas, rhinos can be better protected without such a drastic procedure. Dehorned rhinos are still sometimes poached.

**2** The effects of dehorning have not yet been fully investigated. Dehorning may change the behaviors or social structure of the population. Compared to mothers with horns, mothers without horns may not be able to defend their young calves as well against predators, such as lions or hyenas.

**3** Rhinos may be killed or extremely stressed by the capture, drugging, and dehorning operation.

*Habitat loss is not the biggest cause of the black rhino's decline, as it is with most endangered species. Poaching is the main culprit. Breeding programs are now helping to increase the number of black rhinos in the wild.*

# Moving Rhinos for Protection

In 1970 Kenya was thought to have about 20,000 black rhinos living in the wild. By 1983 fewer than 350 survived. Almost all of them had been killed by poachers for their horns.

As part of a black rhino conservation plan, some rhinos have been moved from less protected areas, where they were in danger of being poached. The rhinos were moved to specially protected rhino sanctuaries in national parks. Transporting and monitoring these rhinos has been expensive. It cost U.S. $12,000 to move ten animals in 1996. Moving rhinos is a complicated procedure. A helicopter team of veterinarians must first find the rhinos and then tranquilize them. They take measurements and small blood and skin samples of each animal for scientific research. The rhinos are then shipped by truck to their new home, where they are kept in special pens to help them adjust to their surroundings. A radio transmitter is then attached to their horns. In this way, scientists can locate them again and check on their health. So far the plan seems to be working. The black rhino herds in Kenya are now increasing slowly. By 1995 Kenya had more than 400 black rhinos.

# Habitat Loss

Habitat loss has not been largely responsible for the drop in black rhino numbers. Habitat loss can explain only a small fraction of the drop in rhino populations over the last few decades. People using land for farming and otherwise destroying the rhino's environment were only partially responsible for the drop in numbers. Even people moving in to establish new farms in rhino habitats probably had a more direct impact by poaching than by farming.

Now that wild black rhino populations are small and separated from one another, even small amounts of habitat loss in these key areas could wipe out a huge percent of the world's black rhino population. Habitat loss in areas protected from people can be caused by drought, floods, fires, and other disasters.

*Conservation organizations are trying to set up breeding groups of black rhinos in countries like Kenya and Zimbabwe.*

# *What You Can Do*

You can help rhinos by learning about them and teaching others
what you have learned. You can also help rhinos by becoming
involved with organizations that protect them. Write to one
of these organizations to learn more about what they are doing
to conserve rhinos. You can also ask them how you can get involved
in protecting rhinos and other wildlife.

## Conservation Groups

### INTERNATIONAL

**International Union for Conservation
of Nature and Natural Resources
(IUCN)**
World Conservation Union
28 rue Mauverney
CH-1196 Gland
Switzerland

**The International Rhino Foundation**
14000 International Rd.
Cumberland, OH
43732
Web site: http://www.IRhinoF.org/

**Save the Rhino International**
105 Park St.
London, W1Y 3FB
United Kingdom

### UNITED STATES

**World Wildlife Fund–United States**
1250 24th St. NW
Washington, D.C.
20037

### CANADA

**World Wildlife Fund–Canada**
90 Eglinton Ave. E.
Suite 504
Toronto, Ontario
M4P 2Z7

# Twenty Fascinating Facts

**1** The rhinoceros got its name from the word *rhino*, which means "nose" in Greek, and *keros*, which means "horned" in Greek.

**2** Even though black rhinos usually have two horns, there have been reports of individuals with three horns or even five horns.

**3** Black rhinos and white rhinos are both gray. The mud and dust baths they take make their skin look like the same color as the dirt. This means rhinos can look brown or red, depending on where they live. The easiest way to tell a black rhino from a white rhino is by the shape of its upper lip.

**4** Rhino horns can grow back if they are knocked off. Young rhinos grow their horns back faster than older animals.

**5** Rhino horn mixed with dried lice is used to treat jaundice in parts of Africa. Jaundice is a blood disorder that gives skin a yellowish tinge.

**6** African rhino horn is more commonly used for medicines in China than in Africa. In Asia, ground-up rhino horn is used to treat fever, convulsions, and many other medical problems.

**7** Rhinos can run quite quickly for their size. They can use their powerful muscles to change direction mid-charge.

**8** In some areas poaching is so hard to stop that armed guards are on 24-hour watch. Some sanctuaries have been fenced to protect black rhinos from poachers.

**9** White rhinos are the biggest of the five rhino species, usually weighing between 5,000 and 7,700 pounds (2,268 and 3,500 kg). Indian rhinos are sometimes taller, but they do not weigh as much. Sumatran rhinos are the smallest, usually weighing less than 1,870 pounds (850 kg).

**10** In 1970 about 65,000 black rhinos lived throughout Africa. Today there are only about 2,500 left. They are now an endangered species.

**11** Rhino horn is not the only part of the rhino that is used in traditional medicines. The hide is also bought and sold. Some zoos even sell rhino urine to treat sore throats and asthma.

**12** Black rhinos regularly sharpen their horns by rubbing them on trees or rocks. Rubbing on rocks wears horns down faster than rubbing on trees.

**13** Rhinos are not usually found in groups. When they are in a group, it is sometimes called a crash of rhinos.

**14** A black rhino mother is very protective of her young. She will even protect her calf against a lion. A young rhino will often stay with its mother for 2 to 5 years, until her next calf is born.

**15** Black rhinos cannot see far, but they have a good sense of smell. Rhinos leave scent marks throughout their own home range. They can tell if a new rhino has been in the area by the scent it leaves behind.

**16** If disturbed, black rhinos may charge at people. They have also been known to charge at vehicles and campfires.

**17** Male black rhinos usually do not fight. They avoid one another by communicating with scent markings. If they do meet, one rhino usually backs down before they even touch.

**18** The rhino's skin is a feeding ground for ticks. More than 20 different species of ticks feed on black rhinos. A bird called the oxpecker rides around on the rhino's back eating the ticks that are feeding off the rhino.

**19** Black rhinos usually eat from the parts of trees or bushes that are close to the ground, but they can reach tree branches that are over 6.6 feet (2 m) high. They eat parts of the branches in addition to the leaves of trees and bushes.

**20** In some cases, black rhinos have been seen eating wildebeest dung. This unusual behavior could mean the rhino is missing important nutrients in its diet that the dung provides.

# Glossary

**browser:** A herbivore that feeds on parts of plants such as leaves or small branches

**crash:** A term used to describe a group of rhinos

**dehorning:** The removal of most of a rhino's horn. This is usually done to make the rhino less attractive to poachers.

**dung:** An animal fecal dropping

**endangered:** A species that is in danger of extinction. Its survival is unlikely if the cause of its decline continues.

**extirpated:** A species that no longer exists in a certain area, but may be found somewhere else

**gestation period:** The length of time a female is pregnant with young

**grazer:** A herbivore that eats all of the plant that is above the ground and sometimes the roots as well

**herbivores:** Animals that eat plants

**home range:** The entire area in which an individual lives

**keratin:** A tough fibrous protein that looks like matted hair. Rhino horns are made of keratin.

**parasites:** Organisms that use other organisms to benefit themselves at the expense of their hosts

**poaching:** A type of hunting that is illegal. Animals, such as rhinos, are often poached for their body parts, which are then sold illegally.

**prehensile:** Specially adapted for gripping objects

**vulnerable:** A species that is likely to become endangered in the future if the cause of its decline continues

**weaned:** When a mammal mother has stopped feeding her milk to her young and the young has learned to eat other food

# Suggested Reading

*African Wildlife Update Newsletter*. African Wildlife News Service. Olympia, Washington. Published bimonthly. Web site: http://www.africanwildlife.org

Kemf, Elizabeth, and Jackson, Peter. *Rhinos in the Wild: A WWF Species Status Report*. Switzerland: World Wide Fund For Nature, 1994.

Martin, Esmond, and Martin, Chrysee Bradley. *Run Rhino Run*. London: Chatto and Windus, 1982.

Martin, Louise. *Rhinoceros: The Wildlife in Danger Series*. Florida: Rourke Enterprises Inc., 1988.

Nowak, Ronald, and Paradiso, John. *Walker's Mammals of the World*. Fourth Edition. Baltimore: John Hopkins University Press, 1983.

Penny, Malcolm. *Rhinos: Endangered Species*. New York: Facts on File, 1988.

Wexo, John. *Rhinos*. Minnesota: Creative Education Inc., 1991.

# Index